The Biography of Elvis Presley

Steven Stafford

Elvis Aaron Presley was an American singer and actor. Regarded as one of the most significant cultural icons of the 20th century, he is often referred to as the "King of Rock and Roll", or simply "the King".

Presley was born in Tupelo, Mississippi, and relocated to Memphis, Tennessee with his family when he was 13 years old. His music career began there in 1954, when he recorded a song with producer Sam Phillips at Sun Records. Accompanied by guitarist Scotty Moore and bassist Bill Black, Presley was an early popularizer of rockabilly, an up-tempo, backbeat-driven fusion of country music and rhythm and blues. RCA Victor acquired his contract in a deal arranged by Colonel Tom Parker, who managed the singer for more than two decades. Presley's first RCA single, "Heartbreak Hotel", was released in January 1956 and became a number-one hit in the United States. He was regarded as the leading figure of rock and roll after a series of successful network television appearances and chart-topping records. His energized interpretations of songs and sexually provocative performance style, combined with a singularly potent mix of influences across color lines that coincided with the dawn of the Civil Rights Movement, made him enormously popular—and controversial.

In November 1956, Presley made his film debut in *Love Me Tender*. In 1958, he was drafted into military service. He resumed his recording career two years later, producing some of his most commercially successful work before devoting much of the 1960s to making Hollywood films and their accompanying soundtrack albums, most of which were critically derided. In 1968, following a seven-year break from live performances, he returned to the stage in the acclaimed televised comeback special *Elvis*, which led to an extended Las Vegas concert residency and a string of highly profitable tours. In 1973, Presley featured in the first globally broadcast concert via satellite, *Aloha from Hawaii*. Several years of prescription drug abuse severely damaged his health, and he died in 1977 at the age of 42.

Presley is one of the most celebrated and influential musicians of the 20th century. Commercially successful in many genres, including pop, blues and gospel, he is one of the best-selling solo artists in the history of recorded music, with estimated record sales of around 600 million units worldwide. He won three Grammys, also receiving the Grammy Lifetime Achievement Award at age 36, and has been inducted into multiple music halls of fame.

1935–1953: Early years

Childhood in Tupelo

Presley was born on January 8, 1935, in Tupelo, Mississippi, to Gladys Love (née Smith; 1912 – 1958) and Vernon Elvis Presley (1916 – 1979), in the two-room shotgun house built by Vernon's father in preparation for the child's birth. Jesse Garon Presley, his identical twin brother, was delivered stillborn 35 minutes before his own birth. Thus, as an only child, Presley became close to both parents and formed an especially close bond with his mother. The family attended an Assembly of God, where he found his initial musical inspiration. Although he was in conflict with the Pentecostal church in his later years, he never officially left it. Rev. Rex Humbard officiated at his funeral, as Presley had been an admirer of Humbard's ministry.

Presley's ancestry was primarily a Western European mix, including Scots-Irish, Scottish, German, and some French Norman. Gladys's great-great-grandmother, Morning Dove White, was possibly a Cherokee Native American. Gladys was regarded by relatives and friends as the dominant member of the small family. Vernon moved from one odd job to the next, evincing little ambition. The family often relied on help from neighbors and government food assistance. The Presleys survived the F5 tornado in the 1936 Tupelo–Gainesville tornado outbreak. In 1938, they lost their home after Vernon was found guilty of kiting a check written by the landowner, Orville S. Bean, the dairy farmer and cattle-and-hog broker for whom he then worked. He was jailed for eight months, and Gladys and Elvis moved in with relatives.

In September 1941, Presley entered first grade at East Tupelo Consolidated, where his instructors regarded him as "average". He was encouraged to enter a singing contest after impressing his schoolteacher with a rendition of Red Foley's country song "Old Shep" during morning prayers. The contest, held at the Mississippi-Alabama Fair and Dairy Show on October 3, 1945, was his first public performance: dressed as a cowboy, the ten-year-old Presley stood on a chair to reach the microphone and sang "Old Shep". He recalled placing fifth. A few months later,

Presley received his first guitar for his birthday; he had hoped for something else—by different accounts, either a bicycle or a rifle. Over the following year, he received basic guitar lessons from two of his uncles and the new pastor at the family's church. Presley recalled, "I took the guitar, and I watched people, and I learned to play a little bit. But I would never sing in public. I was very shy about it."

Entering a new school, Milam, for sixth grade in September 1946, Presley was regarded as a loner. The following year, he began bringing his guitar in on a daily basis. He played and sang during lunchtime, and was often teased as a "trashy" kid who played hillbilly music. The family was by then living in a largely African-American neighborhood. A devotee of Mississippi Slim's show on the Tupelo radio station WELO, Presley was described as "crazy about music" by Slim's younger brother, a classmate of Presley's, who often took him into the station. Slim supplemented Presley's guitar tuition by demonstrating chord techniques. When his protégé was 12 years old, Slim scheduled him for two on-air performances. Presley was overcome by stage fright the first time, but succeeded in performing the following week.

Teenage life in Memphis

In November 1948, the family moved to Memphis, Tennessee. After residing for nearly a year in rooming houses, they were granted a two-bedroom apartment in the public housing complex known as the Lauderdale Courts. Enrolled at L. C. Humes High School, Presley received only a C in music in eighth grade. When his music teacher told him he had no aptitude for singing, he brought in his guitar the next day and sang a recent hit, "Keep Them Cold Icy Fingers Off Me", in an effort to prove otherwise. A classmate later recalled that the teacher "agreed that Elvis was right when he said that she didn't appreciate his kind of singing." He was usually too shy to perform openly, and was occasionally bullied by classmates who viewed him as a "mama's boy". In 1950, he began practicing guitar regularly under the tutelage of Jesse Lee Denson, a neighbor two-and-a-half years his senior. They and three other boys—including two future rockabilly pioneers, brothers Dorsey and Johnny Burnette—formed a loose musical collective that played frequently around the Courts. That September, he began ushering at Loew's State Theater. Other jobs followed, including Precision Tool, Loew's again, and MARL Metal Products.

During his junior year, Presley began to stand out more among his classmates, largely because of his appearance: he grew out his sideburns and styled his hair with rose oil and Vaseline. In his free time, he would head down to Beale Street, the heart of Memphis's thriving blues scene, and gaze longingly at the wild, flashy clothes in the windows of Lansky Brothers. By his senior year, he was wearing them. Overcoming his reticence about performing outside the Lauderdale Courts, he competed in Humes's Annual "Minstrel" show in April 1953. Singing and playing guitar, he opened with "Till I Waltz Again with You", a recent hit for Teresa Brewer. Presley recalled that the performance did much for his reputation: "I wasn't popular in school ... I failed music—only thing I ever failed. And then they entered me in this talent show ... when I came onstage I heard people kind of rumbling and whispering and so forth, 'cause nobody knew I even sang. It was amazing how popular I became after that."

Presley, who never received formal music training or learned to read music, studied and played by ear. He also frequented record stores with jukeboxes and listening booths. He knew all of Hank Snow's songs, and he loved records by other country singers such as Roy Acuff, Ernest Tubb, Ted Daffan, Jimmie Rodgers, Jimmie Davis, and Bob Wills. The Southern gospel singer Jake Hess, one of his favorite performers, was a significant influence on his ballad-singing style. He was a regular audience member at the monthly All-Night Singings downtown, where many of the white gospel groups that performed reflected the influence of African-American spiritual music. He adored the music of black gospel singer Sister Rosetta Tharpe. Like some of his peers, he may have attended blues venues—of necessity, in the segregated South, on only the nights designated for exclusively white audiences. He certainly listened to the regional radio stations, such as WDIA-AM, that played "race records": spirituals, blues, and the modern, backbeat-heavy sound of rhythm and blues. Many of his future recordings were inspired by local African-American musicians such as Arthur Crudup and Rufus Thomas. B.B. King recalled that he had known Presley before he was popular, when they both used to frequent Beale Street. By the time he graduated from high school in June 1953, Presley had already singled out music as his future.

1953–1955: First recordings

Sam Phillips and Sun Records

In August 1953, Presley walked into the offices of Sun
Records. He aimed to pay for a few minutes of studio time
to record a two-sided acetate disc: "My Happiness" and
"That's When Your Heartaches Begin". He would later
claim that he intended the record as a gift for his mother,
or that he was merely interested in what he "sounded
like", although there was a much cheaper, amateur
record-making service at a nearby general store.
Biographer Peter Guralnick argues that he chose Sun in the
hope of being discovered. Asked by receptionist Marion
Keisker what kind of singer he was, Presley responded, "I
sing all kinds." When she pressed him on who he sounded
like, he repeatedly answered, "I don't sound like nobody."
After he recorded, Sun boss Sam Phillips asked Keisker to
note down the young man's name, which she did along
with her own commentary: "Good ballad singer. Hold."

In January 1954, Presley cut a second acetate at Sun
Records—"I'll Never Stand in Your Way" and "It Wouldn't
Be the Same Without You"—but again nothing came of it.
Not long after, he failed an audition for a local vocal
quartet, the Songfellows. He explained to his father, "They
told me I couldn't sing." Songfellow Jim Hamill later
claimed that he was turned down because he did not
demonstrate an ear for harmony at the time. In April,
Presley began working for the Crown Electric company as a
truck driver. His friend Ronnie Smith, after playing a few

local gigs with him, suggested he contact Eddie Bond, leader of Smith's professional band, which had an opening for a vocalist. Bond rejected him after a tryout, advising Presley to stick to truck driving "because you're never going to make it as a singer".

Phillips, meanwhile, was always on the lookout for someone who could bring to a broader audience the sound of the black musicians on whom Sun focused. As Keisker reported, "Over and over I remember Sam saying, 'If I could find a white man who had the Negro sound and the Negro feel, I could make a billion dollars.'" In June, he acquired a demo recording of a ballad, "Without You", that he thought might suit the teenage singer. Presley came by the studio, but was unable to do it justice. Despite this, Phillips asked Presley to sing as many numbers as he knew. He was sufficiently affected by what he heard to invite two local musicians, guitarist Winfield "Scotty" Moore and upright bass player Bill Black, to work something up with Presley for a recording session.

The session, held the evening of July 5, 1954, proved entirely unfruitful until late in the night. As they were about to give up and go home, Presley took his guitar and launched into a 1946 blues number, Arthur Crudup's "That's All Right". Moore recalled, "All of a sudden, Elvis just started singing this song, jumping around and acting the fool, and then Bill picked up his bass, and he started acting the fool, too, and I started playing with them. Sam, I think, had the door to the control booth open ... he stuck his head out and said, 'What are you doing?' And we said, 'We don't know.' 'Well, back up,' he said, 'try to find a place to start, and do it again.'" Phillips quickly began taping; this was the sound he had been looking for. Three days later, popular Memphis DJ Dewey Phillips played "That's All Right" on his Red, Hot, and Blue show. Listeners began phoning in, eager to find out who the singer was. The interest was such that Phillips played the record repeatedly during the last two hours of his show. Interviewing Presley on-air, Phillips asked him what high school he attended in order to clarify his color for the many callers who had assumed he was black. During the next few days, the trio recorded a bluegrass number, Bill Monroe's "Blue Moon of Kentucky", again in a distinctive style and employing a jury-rigged echo effect that Sam Phillips dubbed "slapback". A single was pressed with "That's All Right" on the A side and "Blue Moon of Kentucky" on the reverse.

Early live performances and signing with RCA

The trio played publicly for the first time on July 17 at the Bon Air club—Presley still sporting his child-size guitar. At the end of the month, they appeared at the Overton Park Shell, with Slim Whitman headlining. A combination of his strong response to rhythm and nervousness at playing before a large crowd led Presley to shake his legs as he performed: his wide-cut pants emphasized his movements, causing young women in the audience to start screaming. Moore recalled, "During the instrumental parts, he would back off from the mike and be playing and shaking, and the crowd would just go wild". Black, a natural showman, whooped and rode his bass, hitting double licks that Presley would later remember as "really a wild sound, like a jungle drum or something". Soon after, Moore and Black quit their old band to play with Presley regularly, and DJ and promoter Bob Neal became the trio's manager. From August through October, they played frequently at the Eagle's Nest club and returned to Sun Studio for more recording sessions, and Presley quickly grew more confident on stage. According to Moore, "His movement was a natural thing, but he was also very conscious of what got a reaction. He'd do something one time and then he would expand on it real quick." Presley made what would be his only appearance on Nashville's Grand Ole Opry on October 2; after a polite audience response, Opry manager Jim Denny told Phillips that his singer was "not bad" but did not suit the program. Two weeks later, Presley was booked on Louisiana Hayride, the Opry's chief, and more adventurous, rival. The Shreveport-based show was broadcast to 198 radio stations in 28 states. Presley had another attack of nerves during the first set, which drew a muted reaction. A more composed and energetic second set inspired an enthusiastic response. House drummer D. J. Fontana brought a new element, complementing Presley's movements with accented beats that he had mastered playing in strip clubs. Soon after the show, the Hayride engaged Presley for a year's worth of Saturday-night appearances. Trading in his old guitar for $8 (and seeing it promptly dispatched to the garbage), he purchased a Martin instrument for $175, and his trio began playing in new locales including Houston, Texas, and Texarkana, Arkansas.

By early 1955, Presley's regular Hayride appearances, constant touring, and well-received record releases had made him a regional star, from Tennessee to West Texas. In January, Neal signed a formal management contract with Presley and brought the singer to the attention of Colonel Tom Parker, whom he considered the best promoter in the music business. Having successfully managed top country star Eddy Arnold, Parker was now working with the new number-one country singer, Hank Snow. Parker booked Presley on Snow's February tour. When the tour reached Odessa, Texas, a 19-year-old Roy Orbison saw Presley for the first time: "His energy was incredible, his instinct was just amazing. ... I just didn't know what to make of it. There was just no reference point in the culture to compare it." Presley made his television debut on March 3 on the KSLA-TV broadcast of *Louisiana Hayride*. Soon after, he failed an audition for *Arthur Godfrey's Talent Scouts* on the CBS television network. By August, Sun had released ten sides credited to "Elvis Presley, Scotty and Bill"; on the latest recordings, the trio were joined by a drummer. Some of the songs, like "That's All Right", were in what one Memphis journalist described as the "R&B idiom of negro field jazz"; others, like "Blue Moon of Kentucky", were "more in the country field", "but there was a curious blending of the two different music's in both". This blend of styles made it difficult for Presley's music to find radio airplay. According to Neal, many country-music disc jockeys would not play it because he sounded too much like a black artist and none of the rhythm-and-blues stations would touch him because "he sounded too much like a hillbilly." The blend came to be known as rockabilly. At the time, Presley was variously billed as "The King of Western Bop", "The Hillbilly Cat", and "The Memphis Flash".

Presley renewed Neal's management contract in August 1955, simultaneously appointing Parker as his special adviser. The group maintained an extensive touring schedule throughout the second half of the year. Neal recalled, "It was almost frightening, the reaction that came to Elvis from the teenaged boys. So many of them, through some sort of jealousy, would practically hate him. There were occasions in some towns in Texas when we'd have to be sure to have a police guard because somebody'd always try to take a crack at him. They'd get a gang and try to waylay him or something." The trio became a quartet when Hayride drummer Fontana joined as a full member. In mid-October, they played a few shows in support of Bill Haley, whose "Rock Around the Clock" had been a number-one hit the previous year. Haley observed that Presley had a natural feel for rhythm, and advised him to sing fewer ballads.

At the Country Disc Jockey Convention in early November, Presley was voted the year's most promising male artist. Several record companies had by now shown interest in signing him. After three major labels made offers of up to $25,000, Parker and Phillips struck a deal with RCA Victor on November 21 to acquire Presley's Sun contract for an unprecedented $40,000. Presley, at 20, was still a minor, so his father signed the contract. Parker arranged with the owners of Hill and Range Publishing, Jean and Julian Aberbach, to create two entities, Elvis Presley Music and

Gladys Music, to handle all the new material recorded by Presley. Songwriters were obliged to forgo one third of their customary royalties in exchange for having him perform their compositions. By December, RCA had begun to heavily promote its new singer, and before month's end had reissued many of his Sun recordings.

1956–1958: Commercial breakout and controversy

First national TV appearances and debut album

On January 10, 1956, Presley made his first recordings for RCA in Nashville. Extending the singer's by now customary backup of Moore, Black, and Fontana, RCA enlisted pianist Floyd Cramer, guitarist Chet Atkins, and three background singers, including first tenor Gordon Stoker of the popular Jordanaires quartet, to fill out the sound. The session produced the moody, unusual "Heartbreak Hotel", released as a single on January 27. Parker finally brought Presley to national television, booking him on CBS's *Stage Show* for six appearances over two months. The program, produced in New York, was hosted on alternate weeks by big band leaders and brothers Tommy and Jimmy Dorsey. After his first appearance, on January 28, introduced by disc jockey Bill Randle, Presley stayed in town to record at RCA's New York studio. The sessions yielded eight songs, including a cover of Carl Perkins' rockabilly anthem "Blue Suede Shoes". In February, Presley's "I Forgot to Remember to Forget", a Sun recording initially released the previous August, reached the top of the Billboard country chart. Neal's contract was terminated and, on March 2, Parker became Presley's manager.

On March 12, 1956, Elvis purchased a one-story ranch-style house with two-car attached garage in a quiet residential neighborhood on Audubon Street in Memphis. The home was profiled in national magazines, and soon became a focal point for fans, media and celebrities to visit. Elvis lived here with his parents between March 1956 and March 1957.

RCA Victor released Presley's eponymous debut album on March 23. Joined by five previously unreleased Sun recordings, its seven recently recorded tracks were of a broad variety. There were two country songs and a bouncy pop tune. The others would centrally define the evolving sound of rock and roll: "Blue Suede Shoes"—"an improvement over Perkins' in almost every way", according to critic Robert Hilburn—and three R&B numbers that had been part of Presley's stage repertoire for some time, covers of Little Richard, Ray Charles, and The Drifters. As described by Hilburn, these "were the most revealing of all. Unlike many white artists ... who watered down the gritty edges of the original R&B versions of songs in the '50s, Presley reshaped them. He not only injected the tunes with his own vocal character but also made guitar, not piano, the lead instrument in all three cases." It became the first rock-and-roll album to top the Billboard chart, a position it held for 10 weeks. While Presley was not an innovative guitarist like Moore or contemporary African American rockers Bo Diddley and

Chuck Berry, cultural historian Gilbert B. Rodman argues that the album's cover image, "of Elvis having the time of his life on stage with a guitar in his hands played a crucial role in positioning the guitar ... as the instrument that best captured the style and spirit of this new music."

Milton Berle Show and "Hound Dog"

Presley made the first of two appearances on NBC's *Milton Berle Show* on April 3. His performance, on the deck of the USS Hancock in San Diego, prompted cheers and screams from an audience of sailors and their dates. A few days later, a flight taking Presley and his band to Nashville for a recording session left all three badly shaken when an engine died and the plane almost went down over Arkansas. Twelve weeks after its original release, "Heartbreak Hotel" became Presley's first number-one pop hit. In late April, Presley began a two-week residency at the New Frontier Hotel and Casino on the Las Vegas Strip. The shows were poorly received by the conservative, middle-aged hotel guests—"like a jug of corn liquor at a champagne party," wrote a critic for Newsweek. Amid his Vegas tenure, Presley, who had serious acting ambitions, signed a seven-year contract with Paramount Pictures. He began a tour of the Midwest in mid-May, taking in 15 cities in as many days. He had attended several shows by Freddie Bell and the Bellboys in Vegas and was struck by their cover of "Hound Dog", a hit in 1953 for blues singer Big Mama Thornton by songwriters Jerry Leiber and Mike Stoller. It became the new closing number of his act. After a show in La Crosse, Wisconsin, an urgent message on the letterhead of the local Catholic diocese's newspaper was sent to FBI director J. Edgar Hoover. It warned that "Presley is a definite danger to the security of the United States. ... actions and motions were such as to rouse the sexual passions of teenaged youth. ... After the show, more than 1,000 teenagers tried to gang into Presley's room at the auditorium. ... Indications of the harm Presley did just in La Crosse were the two high school girls ... whose abdomen and thigh had Presley's autograph."

The second *Milton Berle Show* appearance came on June 5 at NBC's Hollywood studio, amid another hectic tour. Berle persuaded the singer to leave his guitar backstage, advising, "Let 'em see you, son." During the performance, Presley abruptly halted an up-tempo rendition of "Hound Dog" with a wave of his arm and launched into a slow, grinding version accentuated with energetic, exaggerated body movements. Presley's gyrations created a storm of controversy. Newspaper critics were outraged: Jack Gould of The New York Times wrote, "Mr. Presley has no discernible singing ability. ... His phrasing, if it can be called that, consists of the stereotyped variations that go with a beginner's aria in a bathtub. ... His one specialty is an accented movement of the body ... primarily identified with the repertoire of the blond bombshells of the burlesque runway." Ben Gross of the New York Daily News opined that popular music "has reached its lowest depths in the 'grunt and groin' antics of one Elvis Presley. ... Elvis, who rotates his pelvis ... gave an exhibition that was suggestive and vulgar, tinged with the kind of animalism that should be confined to dives and bordellos". Ed Sullivan, whose own variety show was the nation's most popular, declared him "unfit for family viewing". To Presley's displeasure, he soon found himself being referred to as "Elvis the Pelvis", which he called "one of the most childish expressions I ever heard, comin' from an adult."

Steve Allen Show and first Sullivan appearance

The Berle shows drew such high ratings that Presley was booked for a July 1 appearance on NBC's *Steve Allen Show* in New York. Allen, no fan of rock and roll, introduced a "new Elvis" in a white bow tie and black tails. Presley sang "Hound Dog" for less than a minute to a basset hound wearing a top hat and bow tie. As described by television historian Jake Austen, "Allen thought Presley was talentless and absurd ... set things up so that Presley would show his contrition". Allen, for his part, later wrote that he found Presley's "strange, gangly, country-boy charisma, his hard-to-define cuteness, and his charming eccentricity intriguing" and simply worked the singer into the customary "comedy fabric" of his program. Just before the final rehearsal for the show, Presley told a reporter, "I'm holding down on this show. I don't want to do anything to make people dislike me. I think TV is important so I'm going to go along, but I won't be able to give the kind of show I do in a personal appearance." Presley would refer back to the Allen show as the most ridiculous performance of his career. Later that night, he appeared on *Hy Gardner Calling*, a popular local TV show. Pressed on whether he had learned anything from the criticism to which he was being subjected, Presley responded, "No, I haven't, I don't feel like I'm doing anything wrong. ... I don't see how any type of music would have any bad influence on people when it's only music. ... I mean, how would rock 'n' roll music make anyone rebel against their parents?"

The next day, Presley recorded "Hound Dog", along with "Any Way You Want Me" and "Don't Be Cruel". The Jordanaires sang harmony, as they had on *The Steve Allen Show*; they would work with Presley through the 1960s. A few days later, the singer made an outdoor concert appearance in Memphis at which he announced, "You know, those people in New York are not gonna change me none. I'm gonna show you what the real Elvis is like tonight." In August, a judge in Jacksonville, Florida, ordered Presley to tame his act. Throughout the following performance, he largely kept still, except for wiggling his little finger suggestively in mockery of the order. The single pairing "Don't Be Cruel" with "Hound Dog" ruled the top of the charts for 11 weeks—a mark that would not be surpassed for 36 years. Recording sessions for Presley's second album took place in Hollywood during the first week of September. Leiber and Stoller, the writers of "Hound Dog," contributed "Love Me."

Allen's show with Presley had, for the first time, beaten CBS's *Ed Sullivan Show* in the ratings. Sullivan, despite his June pronouncement, booked the singer for three appearances for an unprecedented $50,000. The first, on September 9, 1956, was seen by approximately 60 million viewers—a record 82.6 percent of the television audience. Actor Charles Laughton hosted the show, filling in while

Sullivan recuperated from a car accident. Presley appeared in two segments that night from CBS Television City in Los Angeles. According to Elvis legend, Presley was shot from only the waist up. Watching clips of the Allen and Berle shows with his producer, Sullivan had opined that Presley "got some kind of device hanging down below the crotch of his pants—so when he moves his legs back and forth you can see the outline of his cock. ... I think it's a Coke bottle. ... We just can't have this on a Sunday night. This is a family show!" Sullivan publicly told TV Guide, "As for his gyrations, the whole thing can be controlled with camera shots." In fact, Presley was shown head-to-toe in the first and second shows. Though the camerawork was relatively discreet during his debut, with leg-concealing closeups when he danced, the studio audience reacted in customary style: screaming. Presley's performance of his forthcoming single, the ballad "Love Me Tender", prompted a record-shattering million advance orders. More than any other single event, it was this first appearance on *The Ed Sullivan Show* that made Presley a national celebrity of barely precedented proportions.

Accompanying Presley's rise to fame, a cultural shift was taking place that he both helped inspire and came to symbolize. Igniting the "biggest pop craze since Glenn Miller and Frank Sinatra ... Presley brought Rock'n'Roll into the mainstream of popular culture", writes historian Marty Jezer. "As Presley set the artistic pace, other artists followed. ... Presley, more than anyone else, gave the young a belief in themselves as a distinct and somehow unified generation—the first in America ever to feel the power of an integrated youth culture."

Crazed crowds and film debut

The audience response at Presley's live shows became increasingly fevered. Moore recalled, "He'd start out, 'You ain't nothin' but a Hound Dog,' and they'd just go to pieces. They'd always react the same way. There'd be a riot every time." At the two concerts he performed in September at the Mississippi-Alabama Fair and Dairy Show, 50 National Guardsmen were added to the police security to prevent crowd trouble. Elvis, Presley's second album, was released in October and quickly rose to number one. The album includes "Old Shep", which he sang at the talent show in 1945, and which now marked the first time he played piano on an RCA session. According to Guralnick, one can hear "in the halting chords and the somewhat stumbling rhythm both the unmistakable emotion and the equally unmistakable valuing of emotion over technique." Assessing the musical and cultural impact of Presley's recordings from "That's All Right" through Elvis, rock critic Dave Marsh wrote that "these records, more than any others, contain the seeds of what rock & roll was, has been and most likely what it may foreseeably become."

Presley returned to the Sullivan show at its main studio in New York, hosted this time by its namesake, on October 28. After the performance, crowds in Nashville and St. Louis burned him in effigy. His first motion picture, Love Me Tender, was released on November 21. Though he was not top billed, the film's original title—The Reno Brothers—was changed to capitalize on his latest number one record: "Love Me Tender" had hit the top of the charts earlier that month. To further take advantage of Presley's popularity, four musical numbers were added to what was originally a straight acting role. The film was panned by the critics but did very well at the box office.

On December 4, Presley dropped into Sun Records where Carl Perkins and Jerry Lee Lewis were recording and jammed with them. Though Phillips no longer had the right to release any Presley material, he made sure the session was captured on tape. The results became legendary as the "Million Dollar Quartet" recordings—Johnny Cash was long thought to have played as well, but he was present only briefly at Phillips' instigation for a photo opportunity. The year ended with a front-page story in The Wall Street Journal reporting that Presley merchandise had brought in $22 million on top of his record sales, and Billboard's declaration that he had placed more songs in the top 100 than any other artist since records were first charted. In his first full year at RCA, one of the music industry's largest companies, Presley had accounted for over 50 percent of the label's singles sales.

Leiber and Stoller collaboration and draft notice

Presley made his third and final *Ed Sullivan Show* appearance on January 6, 1957—on this occasion indeed shot only down to the waist. Some commentators have claimed that Parker orchestrated an appearance of censorship to generate publicity. In any event, as critic Greil Marcus describes, Presley "did not tie himself down. Leaving behind the bland clothes he had worn on the first two shows, he stepped out in the outlandish costume of a pasha, if not a harem girl. From the make-up over his eyes, the hair falling in his face, the overwhelmingly sexual cast of his mouth, he was playing Rudolph Valentino in The Sheik, with all stops out." To close, displaying his range and defying Sullivan's wishes, Presley sang a gentle black spiritual, "Peace in the Valley". At the end of the show, Sullivan declared Presley "a real decent, fine boy". Two days later, the Memphis draft board announced that Presley would be classified 1-A and would probably be drafted sometime that year.

Each of the three Presley singles released in the first half of 1957 went to number one: "Too Much", "All Shook Up", and "(Let Me Be Your) Teddy Bear". Already an international star, he was attracting fans even where his music was not officially released. Under the headline "Presley Records a Craze in Soviet", The New York Times reported that pressings of his music on discarded X-ray plates were commanding high prices in Leningrad. Between film shoots and recording sessions, the singer also found time to purchase an 18-room mansion eight miles (13 km) south of downtown Memphis for himself and his parents: Graceland. When he reported to the film studio for his second film, the Technicolor *Loving You*, released in July, "The makeup man said that with his eyes he should photograph well with black hair, so they dyed it." Loving You, the accompanying soundtrack, was Presley's third straight number one album. The title track was written by Leiber and Stoller, who were then retained to write four of the six songs recorded at the sessions for Jailhouse Rock, Presley's next film. The songwriting team effectively produced the Jailhouse sessions and developed a close working relationship with Presley, who came to regard them as his "good-luck charm".

Leiber remembered initially finding Presley "not quite authentic—after all, he was a white singer, and my standards were black." According to Stoller, the duo was "surprised at the kind of knowledge that he had about black music. We figured that he had these remarkable pipes and all that, but we didn't realize that he knew so much about the blues. We were quite surprised to find out that he knew as much about it as we did. He certainly knew a lot more than we did about country music and gospel music." Leiber remembered the recording process with Presley, "He was fast. Any demo you gave him he knew by heart in ten minutes." As Stoller recalled, Presley "was 'protected'" by his manager and entourage. "He was removed. ... They kept him separate."

Presley undertook three brief tours during the year, continuing to generate a crazed audience response. A Detroit newspaper suggested that "the trouble with going to see Elvis Presley is that you're liable to get killed." Villanova students pelted him with eggs in Philadelphia, and in Vancouver, the crowd rioted after the end of the show, destroying the stage. Frank Sinatra, who had famously inspired the swooning of teenaged girls in the 1940s, condemned the new musical phenomenon. In a magazine article, he decried rock and roll as "brutal, ugly, degenerate, vicious. ... It fosters almost totally negative and destructive reactions in young people. It smells phoney and false. It is sung, played and written, for the most part, by cretinous goons. ... This rancid-smelling aphrodisiac I deplore." Asked for a response, Presley said, "I admire the man. He has a right to say what he wants to say. He is a great success and a fine actor, but I think he shouldn't have said it. ... This is a trend, just the same as he faced when he started years ago."

Leiber and Stoller were again in the studio for the recording of Elvis' Christmas Album. Toward the end of the session, they wrote a song on the spot at Presley's request: "Santa Claus Is Back in Town", an innuendo-laden blues. The holiday release stretched Presley's string of number one albums to four and would eventually become the bestselling Christmas album of all time. After the session, Moore and Black—drawing only modest weekly salaries, sharing in none of Presley's massive financial success—resigned. Though they were brought back on a per diem basis a few weeks later, it was clear that they had not been part of Presley's inner circle for some time. On December 20, Presley received his draft notice. He was granted a deferment to finish the forthcoming King Creole, in which $350,000 had already been invested by Paramount and producer Hal Wallis. A couple of weeks into the new year, "Don't", another Leiber and Stoller tune, became Presley's tenth number one seller. It had been only 21 months since "Heartbreak Hotel" had brought him to the top for the first time. Recording sessions for the King Creole soundtrack were held in Hollywood mid-January. Leiber and Stoller provided three songs and were again on hand, but it would be the last time they worked closely with Presley. A studio session on February 1 marked another ending: it was the final occasion on which Black was to perform with Presley. He died in 1965.

1958–1960: Military service and mother's death

On March 24, 1958, Presley was conscripted into the U.S. Army as a private at Fort Chaffee, near Fort Smith, Arkansas. His arrival was a major media event. Hundreds of people descended on Presley as he stepped from the bus; photographers then accompanied him into the fort. Presley announced that he was looking forward to his military stint, saying he did not want to be treated any differently from anyone else: "The Army can do anything it wants with me."

Soon after Presley commenced basic training at Fort Hood, Texas, he received a visit from Eddie Fadal, a businessman he had met on tour. According to Fadal, Presley had become convinced his career was finished—"He firmly believed that." But then, during a two-week leave in early June, Presley recorded five songs in Nashville. In early August, his mother was diagnosed with hepatitis and her condition rapidly worsened. Presley, granted emergency leave to visit her, arrived in Memphis on August 12. Two days later, she died of heart failure, aged 46. Presley was devastated; their relationship had remained extremely close—even into his adulthood, they would use baby talk with each other and Presley would address her with pet names.

After training, Presley joined the 3rd Armored Division in Friedberg, Germany, on October 1. Introduced to amphetamines by a sergeant while on maneuvers, he became "practically evangelical about their benefits"—not only for energy, but for "strength" and weight loss, as well—and many of his friends in the outfit joined him in indulging. The Army also introduced Presley to karate, which he studied seriously, later including it in his live performances. Fellow soldiers have attested to Presley's wish to be seen as an able, ordinary soldier, despite his fame, and to his generosity. He donated his Army pay to charity, purchased TV sets for the base, and bought an extra set of fatigues for everyone in his outfit.

While in Friedberg, Presley met 14-year-old Priscilla Beaulieu. They would eventually marry after a seven-and-a-half-year courtship. In her autobiography, Priscilla says that despite his worries that it would ruin his career, Parker convinced Presley that to gain popular respect, he should serve his country as a regular soldier rather than in Special Services, where he would have been able to give some musical performances and remain in touch with the public. Media reports echoed Presley's concerns about his career, but RCA producer Steve Sholes and Freddy Bienstock of Hill and Range had carefully prepared for his two-year hiatus. Armed with a substantial amount of unreleased material, they kept up a regular stream of successful releases. Between his induction and discharge, Presley had ten top 40 hits, including "Wear My Ring Around Your Neck", the best-selling "Hard Headed Woman", and "One Night" in 1958, and "(Now and Then There's) A Fool Such as I" and the number one "A Big Hunk o' Love" in 1959. RCA also generated four albums compiling old material during this period, most successfully Elvis' Golden Records (1958), which hit number three on the LP chart.

1960–1967: Focus on films

Elvis Is Back

Presley returned to the United States on March 2, 1960, and was honorably discharged with the rank of sergeant on March 5. The train that carried him from New Jersey to Tennessee was mobbed all the way, and Presley was called upon to appear at scheduled stops to please his fans. On the night of March 20, he entered RCA's Nashville studio to cut tracks for a new album along with a single, "Stuck on You", which was rushed into release and swiftly became a number one hit. Another Nashville session two weeks later yielded a pair of his best-selling singles, the ballads "It's Now or Never" and "Are You Lonesome Tonight?", along with the rest of Elvis Is Back! The album features several songs described by Greil Marcus as full of Chicago blues "menace, driven by Presley's own super-miked acoustic guitar, brilliant playing by Scotty Moore, and demonic sax work from Boots Randolph. Elvis's singing wasn't sexy, it was pornographic." As a whole, the record "conjured up the vision of a performer who could be all things", in the words of music historian John Robertson: "a flirtatious teenage idol with a heart of gold; a tempestuous, dangerous lover; a gutbucket blues singer; a sophisticated nightclub entertainer; raucous rocker".

Presley returned to television on May 12 as a guest *on The Frank Sinatra Timex Special*—ironic for both stars, given Sinatra's not-so-distant excoriation of rock and roll. Also known as *Welcome Home Elvis*, the show had been taped in late March, the only time all year Presley performed in front of an audience. Parker secured an unheard-of $125,000 fee for eight minutes of singing. The broadcast drew an enormous viewership.

G.I. Blues, the soundtrack to Presley's first film since his return, was a number one album in October. His first LP of sacred material, His Hand in Mine, followed two months later. It reached number 13 on the U.S. pop chart and number 3 in the UK, remarkable figures for a gospel album. In February 1961, Presley performed two shows for a benefit event in Memphis, on behalf of 24 local charities. During a luncheon preceding the event, RCA presented him with a plaque certifying worldwide sales of over 75 million records. A 12-hour Nashville session in mid-March yielded nearly all of Presley's next studio album, Something for Everybody. As described by John Robertson, it exemplifies the Nashville sound, the restrained, cosmopolitan style that would define country music in the 1960s. Presaging much of what was to come from Presley himself over the next half-decade, the album is largely "a pleasant, unthreatening pastiche of the music that had once been Elvis's birthright." It would be his sixth number one LP. Another benefit concert, raising money for a Pearl Harbor memorial, was staged on March 25, in Hawaii. It was to be Presley's last public performance for seven years.

Lost in Hollywood

Parker had by now pushed Presley into a heavy film making schedule, focused on formulaic, modestly budgeted musical comedies. Presley at first insisted on pursuing more serious roles, but when two films in a more dramatic vein—*Flaming Star* (1960) and *Wild in the Country* (1961)—were less commercially successful, he reverted to the formula. Among the 27 films he made during the 1960s, there were few further exceptions. His films were almost universally panned; critic Andrew Caine dismissed them as a "pantheon of bad taste". Nonetheless, they were virtually all profitable. Hal Wallis, who produced nine of them, declared, "A Presley picture is the only sure thing in Hollywood."

Of Presley's films in the 1960s, 15 were accompanied by soundtrack albums and another 5 by soundtrack EPs. The films' rapid production and release schedules—he frequently starred in three a year—affected his music. According to Jerry Leiber, the soundtrack formula was already evident before Presley left for the Army: "three ballads, one medium-tempo [number], one up-tempo, and one break blues boogie". As the decade wore on, the quality of the soundtrack songs grew "progressively worse". Julie Parrish, who appeared in *Paradise, Hawaiian Style* (1966), says that he hated many of the songs chosen for his films. The Jordanaires' Gordon Stoker describes how Presley would retreat from the studio microphone: "The material was so bad that he felt like he couldn't sing it." Most of the film albums featured a song or two from respected writers such as the team of Doc Pomus and

Mort Shuman. But by and large, according to biographer Jerry Hopkins, the numbers seemed to be "written on order by men who never really understood Elvis or rock and roll." Regardless of the songs' quality, it has been argued that Presley generally sang them well, with commitment. Critic Dave Marsh heard the opposite: "Presley isn't trying, probably the wisest course in the face of material like 'No Room to Rumba in a Sports Car' and 'Rock-a-Hula Baby.'"

In the first half of the decade, three of Presley's soundtrack albums hit number one on the pop charts, and a few of his most popular songs came from his films, such as "Can't Help Falling in Love" (1961) and "Return to Sender" (1962). ("Viva Las Vegas", the title track to the 1964 film, was a minor hit as a B-side, and became truly popular only later.) But, as with artistic merit, the commercial returns steadily diminished. During a five-year span—1964 through 1968—Presley had only one top-ten hit: "Crying in the Chapel" (1965), a gospel number recorded back in 1960. As for non-film albums, between the June 1962 release of Pot Luck and the November 1968 release of the soundtrack to the television special that signaled his comeback, only one LP of new material by Presley was issued: the gospel album How Great Thou Art (1967). It won him his first Grammy Award, for Best Sacred Performance. As Marsh described, Presley was "arguably the greatest white gospel singer of his time' really the last rock & roll artist to make gospel as vital a component of his musical personality as his secular songs."

Shortly before Christmas 1966, more than seven years since they first met, Presley proposed to Priscilla Beaulieu. They were married on May 1, 1967, in a brief ceremony in their suite at the Aladdin Hotel in Las Vegas. The flow of formulaic films and assembly-line soundtracks rolled on. It was not until October 1967, when the *Clambake* soundtrack LP registered record low sales for a new Presley album, that RCA executives recognized a problem. "By then, of course, the damage had been done", as historians Connie Kirchberg and Marc Hendrickx put it. "Elvis was viewed as a joke by serious music lovers and a has-been to all but his most loyal fans."

1968–1973: Comeback

Elvis: the '68 Comeback Special

Presley's only child, Lisa Marie, was born on February 1, 1968, during a period when he had grown deeply unhappy with his career. Of the eight Presley singles released between January 1967 and May 1968, only two charted in the top 40, and none higher than number 28. His forthcoming soundtrack album, Speedway, would die at number 82 on the Billboard chart. Parker had already shifted his plans to television, where Presley had not appeared since the Sinatra Timex show in 1960. He maneuvered a deal with NBC that committed the network to both finance a theatrical feature and broadcast a Christmas special.

Recorded in late June in Burbank, California, the special, called simply *Elvis,* aired on December 3, 1968. Later known as the *'68 Comeback Special,* the show featured lavishly staged studio productions as well as songs performed with a band in front of a small audience— Presley's first live performances since 1961. The live segments saw Presley clad in tight black leather, singing and playing guitar in an uninhibited style reminiscent of his early rock-and-roll days. Bill Belew, who designed this outfit, gave it a Napoleonic standing collar (Presley customarily wore high collars because he believed his neck looked too long), a design feature that he would later make a major trademark of the outfits Presley wore on stage in his later years. Director and coproducer Steve Binder had worked hard to reassure the nervous singer and to produce a show that was far from the hour of Christmas songs Parker had originally planned. The show, NBC's highest rated that season, captured 42 percent of the total viewing audience. Jon Landau of Eye magazine remarked, "There is something magical about watching a man who has lost himself find his way back home. He sang with the kind of power people no longer expect of rock 'n' roll singers. He moved his body with a lack of pretension and effort that must have made Jim Morrison green with envy." Dave Marsh calls the performance one of "emotional grandeur and historical resonance."

By January 1969, the single "If I Can Dream", written for the special, reached number 12. The soundtrack album broke into the top ten. According to friend Jerry Schilling, the special reminded Presley of what "he had not been able to do for years, being able to choose the people;

being able to choose what songs and not being told what had to be on the soundtrack. ... He was out of prison, man." Binder said of Presley's reaction, "I played Elvis the 60-minute show, and he told me in the screening room, 'Steve, it's the greatest thing I've ever done in my life. I give you my word I will never sing a song I don't believe in.'"

From Elvis In Memphis and the International

Buoyed by the experience of the Comeback Special, Presley engaged in a prolific series of recording sessions at American Sound Studio, which led to the acclaimed From Elvis in Memphis. Released in June 1969, it was his first secular, non-soundtrack album from a dedicated period in the studio in eight years. As described by Dave Marsh, it is "a masterpiece in which Presley immediately catches up with pop music trends that had seemed to pass him by during the movie years. He sings country songs, soul songs and rockers with real conviction, a stunning achievement."

Presley was keen to resume regular live performing. Following the success of the Comeback Special, offers came in from around the world. The London Palladium offered Parker $28,000 for a one-week engagement. He responded, "That's fine for me, now how much can you get for Elvis?" In May, the brand new International Hotel in Las Vegas, boasting the largest showroom in the city, announced that it had booked Presley, scheduling him to perform 57 shows over four weeks beginning July 31. Moore, Fontana, and the Jordanaires declined to participate, afraid of losing the lucrative session work they had in Nashville. Presley assembled new, top-notch accompaniment, led by guitarist James Burton and including two gospel groups, The Imperials and The Sweet Inspirations. Nonetheless, he was nervous: his only previous Las Vegas engagement, in 1956, had been dismal, and he had neither forgotten nor forgiven that failure. To revise his approach to performances, Presley visited Las Vegas hotel showrooms and lounges, at one of which, that of the Flamingo, he encountered Tom Jones, whose aggressive style was similar to his own 1950s approach; the two became friends. Already studying karate at the time, Presley recruited Bill Belew to design variants of karatekas's gis for him; these, in jumpsuit form, would be his "stage uniforms" in his later years. Parker, who intended to make Presley's return the show business event of the year, oversaw a major promotional push. For his part, hotel owner Kirk Kerkorian arranged to send his own plane to New York to fly in rock journalists for the debut performance.

Presley took to the stage without introduction. The audience of 2,200, including many celebrities, gave him a standing ovation before he sang a note and another after his performance. A third followed his encore, "Can't Help Falling in Love" (a song that would be his closing number for much of the 1970s). At a press conference after the show, when a journalist referred to him as "The King", Presley gestured toward Fats Domino, who was taking in the scene. "No," Presley said, "that's the real king of rock and roll." The next day, Parker's negotiations with the hotel resulted in a five-year contract for Presley to play each February and August, at an annual salary of $1 million. Newsweek commented, "There are several unbelievable things about Elvis, but the most incredible is his staying power in a world where meteoric careers fade like shooting stars." Rolling Stone called Presley "supernatural, his own resurrection." In November, Presley's final non-concert film, Change of Habit, opened. The double album From Memphis To Vegas/From Vegas To Memphis came out the same month; the first LP consisted of live performances from the International, the second of more cuts from the American Sound sessions. "Suspicious Minds" reached the top of the charts— Presley's first U.S. pop number one in over seven years, and his last.

Cassandra Peterson, later television's Elvira, met Presley during this period in Las Vegas, where she was working as a showgirl. She recalls of their encounter, "He was so anti-drug when I met him. I mentioned to him that I smoked marijuana, and he was just appalled. He said, 'Don't ever do that again.'" Presley was not only deeply opposed to recreational drugs, he also rarely drank. Several of his family members had been alcoholics, a fate he intended to avoid.

Back on tour and meeting Nixon

Presley returned to the International early in 1970 for the first of the year's two month-long engagements, performing two shows a night. Recordings from these shows were issued on the album On Stage. In late

February, Presley performed six attendance-record–breaking shows at the Houston Astrodome. In April, the single "The Wonder of You" was issued—a number one hit in the UK, it topped the U.S. adult contemporary chart, as well. MGM filmed rehearsal and concert footage at the International during August for the documentary Elvis: That's the Way It Is. Presley was by now performing in a jumpsuit, which would become a trademark of his live act. During this engagement, he was threatened with murder unless $50,000 was paid. Presley had been the target of many threats since the 1950s, often without his knowledge. The FBI took the threat seriously and security was stepped up for the next two shows. Presley went onstage with a Derringer in his right boot and a .45 pistol in his waistband, but the concerts went off without incident.

The album That's the Way It Is, produced to accompany the documentary and featuring both studio and live recordings, marked a stylistic shift. As music historian John Robertson notes, "The authority of Presley's singing helped disguise the fact that the album stepped decisively away from the American-roots inspiration of the Memphis sessions towards a more middle-of-the-road sound. With country put on the back burner, and soul and R&B left in Memphis, what was left was very classy, very clean white pop—perfect for the Las Vegas crowd, but a definite retrograde step for Elvis." After the end of his International engagement on September 7, Presley embarked on a week-long concert tour, largely of the South, his first since 1958. Another week-long tour, of the West Coast, followed in November.

On December 21, 1970, Presley engineered a meeting with President Richard Nixon at the White House, where he expressed his patriotism and his contempt for the hippies, the growing drug culture, and the counterculture in general. He asked Nixon for a Bureau of Narcotics and Dangerous Drugs badge, to add to similar items he had begun collecting and to signify official sanction of his patriotic efforts. Nixon, who apparently found the encounter awkward, expressed a belief that Presley could send a positive message to young people and that it was therefore important he "retain his credibility". Presley told Nixon that the Beatles, whose songs he regularly performed in concert during the era, exemplified what he saw as a trend of anti-Americanism and drug abuse in popular culture. On hearing reports of the meeting, Paul McCartney later said he "felt a bit betrayed" and commented: "The great joke was that we were taking [illegal] drugs, and look what happened to him", a reference to Presley's death, hastened by prescription drug abuse.

The U.S. Junior Chamber of Commerce named Presley one of its annual Ten Most Outstanding Young Men of the Nation on January 16, 1971. Not long after, the City of Memphis named the stretch of Highway 51 South on which Graceland is located "Elvis Presley Boulevard". The same year, Presley became the first rock and roll singer to be awarded the Lifetime Achievement Award (then known as the Bing Crosby Award) by the National Academy of Recording Arts and Sciences, the Grammy Award organization. Three new, non-film Presley studio albums were released in 1971, as many as had come out over the previous eight years. Best received by critics was Elvis Country, a concept record that focused on genre standards. The biggest seller was Elvis Sings the Wonderful World of Christmas, "the truest statement of all", according to Greil Marcus. "In the midst of ten painfully genteel Christmas songs, every one sung with appalling sincerity and humility, one could find Elvis tom-catting his way through six blazing minutes of 'Merry Christmas Baby,' a raunchy old Charles Brown blues." According to Guralnick, "the one real highlight" of one of the 1971 sessions were the recording of "I Will Be True," "It's Still Here," and "I'll Take You Home Again, Kathleen," a trio of songs that Presley recorded in a rare solo set, sitting at the piano after everyone else had gone home: "Yearning, wistfulness, loneliness, need—all were communicated with a naked lack of adornment that Elvis was seeming to find increasingly difficult to display in the formal process of recording."

Marriage breakdown and Aloha from Hawaii

MGM again filmed Presley in April 1972, this time for *Elvis on Tour*, which went on to win the Golden Globe Award for Best Documentary Film that year. His gospel album He Touched Me, released that month, would earn him his second Grammy Award, for Best Inspirational Performance. A 14-date tour commenced with an unprecedented four consecutive sold-out shows at New York's Madison Square Garden. The evening concert on July 10 was recorded and issued in LP form a week later. Elvis: As Recorded at Madison Square Garden became one of Presley's biggest-selling albums. After the tour, the single "Burning Love" was released—Presley's last top ten hit on the U.S. pop chart. "The most exciting single Elvis has made since 'All Shook Up'", wrote rock critic Robert Christgau. "Who else could make 'It's coming closer, the flames are now licking my body' sound like an assignation with James Brown's backup band?"

Presley and his wife, meanwhile, had become increasingly distant, barely cohabiting. In 1971, an affair he had with Joyce Bova resulted—unbeknownst to him—in her pregnancy and an abortion. He often raised the possibility of her moving into Graceland, saying that he was likely to leave Priscilla. The Presleys separated on February 23, 1972, after Priscilla disclosed her relationship with Mike Stone, a karate instructor Presley had recommended to her. Priscilla relates that when she told him, Presley "grabbed ... and forcefully made love to" her, declaring, "This is how a real man makes love to his woman." Five months later, Presley's new girlfriend, Linda Thompson, a songwriter and one-time Memphis beauty queen, moved in with him. Presley and his wife filed for divorce on August 18. According to Joe Moscheo of the Imperials, the failure of Presley's marriage "was a blow from which he never recovered."

In January 1973, Presley performed two benefit concerts for the Kui Lee Cancer Fund in connection with a groundbreaking TV special, *Aloha from Hawaii*. The first show served as a practice run and backup should technical problems affect the live broadcast two days later. Aired as scheduled on January 14, *Aloha from Hawaii* was the first global concert satellite broadcast, reaching millions of viewers live and on tape delay. Presley's costume became the most recognized example of the elaborate concert garb with which his latter-day persona became closely associated. As described by Bobbie Ann Mason, "At the end of the show, when he spreads out his American Eagle cape, with the full stretched wings of the eagle studded on the back, he becomes a god figure." The accompanying double album, released in February, went to number one and eventually sold over 5 million copies in the United States. It proved to be Presley's last U.S. number one pop album during his lifetime.

At a midnight show the same month, four men rushed onto the stage in an apparent attack. Security men leapt to Presley's defense, and the singer's karate instinct took over as he ejected one invader from the stage himself. Following the show, he became obsessed with the idea that the men had been sent by Mike Stone to kill him. Though they were shown to have been only overexuberant fans, he raged, "There's too much pain in me ... Stone die." His outbursts continued with such intensity that a physician was unable to calm him, despite administering large doses of medication. After another two full days of raging, Red West, his friend and bodyguard, felt compelled to get a price for a contract killing and was relieved when Presley decided, "Aw hell, let's just leave it for now. Maybe it's a bit heavy."

1973–1977: Health deterioration and death

Medical crises and last studio sessions

Presley's divorce took effect on October 9, 1973. He was now becoming increasingly unwell. Twice during the year he overdosed on barbiturates, spending three days in a coma in his hotel suite after the first incident. Toward the end of 1973, he was hospitalized, semi comatose from the effects of pethidine addiction. According to his primary care physician, Dr. George C. Nichopoulos, Presley "felt that by getting [drugs] from a doctor, he wasn't the common everyday junkie getting something off the street." Since his comeback, he had staged more live shows with each passing year, and 1973 saw 168 concerts, his busiest schedule ever. Despite his failing health, in 1974 he undertook another intensive touring schedule.

Presley's condition declined precipitously in September. Keyboardist Tony Brown remembers the singer's arrival at a University of Maryland concert: "He fell out of the limousine, to his knees. People jumped to help, and he pushed them away like, 'Don't help me.' He walked on stage and held onto the mike for the first thirty minutes like it was a post. Everybody's looking at each other like, Is the tour gonna happen?" Guitarist John Wilkinson recalled, "He was all gut. He was slurring. He was so fucked up. ... It was obvious he was drugged. It was obvious there was something terribly wrong with his body. It was so bad the words to the songs were barely intelligible. ... I remember crying. He could barely get through the introductions". Wilkinson recounted that a few nights later in Detroit, "I watched him in his dressing room, just draped over a chair, unable to move. So often I thought, 'Boss, why don't you just cancel this tour and take a year off ...?' I mentioned something once in a guarded moment. He patted me on the back and said, 'It'll be all right. Don't you worry about it.'" Presley continued to play to sellout crowds.

On July 13, 1976, Vernon Presley—who had become deeply involved in his son's financial affairs—fired "Memphis Mafia" bodyguards Red West (Presley's friend since the 1950s), Sonny West, and David Hebler, citing the need to "cut back on expenses". Presley was in Palm Springs at the time, and some suggest the singer was too cowardly to face the three himself. Another associate of Presley's, John O'Grady, argued that the bodyguards were dropped because their rough treatment of fans had prompted too many lawsuits. However, Presley's stepbrother David Stanley has claimed that the bodyguards were fired because they were becoming more outspoken about Presley's drug dependency.

RCA, which had enjoyed a steady stream of product from Presley for over a decade, grew anxious as his interest in spending time in the studio waned. After a December 1973 session that produced 18 songs, enough for almost two albums, he did not enter the studio in 1974. Parker sold RCA on another concert record, Elvis Recorded Live on Stage in Memphis. Recorded on March 20, it included a version of "How Great Thou Art" that would win Presley his third and final competitive Grammy Award. (All three of his competitive Grammy wins—out of 14 total nominations—were for gospel recordings.) Presley returned to the studio in Hollywood in March 1975, but Parker's attempts to arrange another session toward the end of the year were unsuccessful. In 1976, RCA sent a mobile studio to Graceland that made possible two full-scale recording sessions at Presley's home. Even in that comfortable context, the recording process was now a struggle for him.

For all the concerns of his label and manager, in studio sessions between July 1973 and October 1976, Presley recorded virtually the entire contents of six albums. Though he was no longer a major presence on the pop charts, five of those albums entered the top five of the country chart, and three went to number one: Promised Land (1975), From Elvis Presley Boulevard, Memphis, Tennessee (1976), and Moody Blue (1977). The story was similar with his singles—there were no major pop hits, but Presley was a significant force in not just the country market, but on adult contemporary radio as well. Eight studio singles from this period released during his lifetime were top ten hits on one or both charts, four in 1974 alone. "My Boy" was a number one adult contemporary hit in 1975, and "Moody Blue" topped the country chart and reached the second spot on the adult contemporary chart in 1976. Perhaps his most critically acclaimed recording of the era came that year, with what Greil Marcus described as his "apocalyptic attack" on the soul classic "Hurt". "If he felt the way he sounded", Dave Marsh wrote of Presley's performance, "the wonder isn't that he had only a year left to live but that he managed to survive that long."

Final year and death

Presley and Linda Thompson split in November 1976, and he took up with a new girlfriend, Ginger Alden. He proposed to Alden and gave her an engagement ring two months later, though several of his friends later claimed that he had no serious intention of marrying again. Journalist Tony Scherman writes that by early 1977, "Presley had become a grotesque caricature of his sleek, energetic former self. Hugely overweight, his mind dulled by the pharmacopeia he daily ingested, he was barely able to pull himself through his abbreviated concerts." In Alexandria, Louisiana, the singer was on stage for less than an hour and "was impossible to understand". Presley failed to appear in Baton Rouge; he was unable to get out of his hotel bed, and the rest of the tour was cancelled. Despite the accelerating deterioration of his health, he stuck to most touring commitments. In Rapid City, South Dakota, "he was so nervous on stage that he could hardly talk", according to Presley historian Samuel Roy, and unable to "perform any significant movement." Guralnick relates that fans "were becoming increasingly voluble about their disappointment, but it all seemed to go right past Presley, whose world was now confined almost entirely to his room and his spiritualism books." A cousin, Billy Smith, recalled how Presley would sit in his room and chat for hours, sometimes recounting favorite Monty Python sketches and his own past escapades, but more often gripped by paranoid obsessions that reminded Smith of Howard Hughes. "Way Down", Presley's last single issued during his lifetime, came out on June 6. On the next tour, CBS filmed two concerts for a TV Special, *Elvis in Concert*, to be aired in October. On the first of these, captured in Omaha on June 19, Presley's voice, Guralnick writes, "is almost unrecognizable, a small, childlike instrument in which he talks more than sings most of the songs, casts about uncertainly for the melody in others, and is virtually unable to articulate or project." He did better on the second night, two days later in Rapid City: "He looked healthier, seemed to have lost a little weight, and sounded better, too", though his appearance was still a "face framed in a helmet of blue-black hair from which sweat sheets down over pale, swollen cheeks." His final concert was held in Indianapolis, Indiana at Market Square Arena, on June 26.

The book Elvis: What Happened?, cowritten by the three bodyguards fired the previous year, was published on August 1. It was the first exposé to detail Presley's years of drug misuse. He was devastated by the book and tried unsuccessfully to halt its release by offering money to the publishers. By this point, he suffered from multiple ailments: glaucoma, high blood pressure, liver damage, and an enlarged colon, each aggravated—and possibly caused—by drug abuse. Genetic analysis of a hair sample in 2014 found evidence of genetic variants that could have caused his glaucoma, migraines and hypertrophic cardiomyopathy.

Presley was scheduled to fly out of Memphis on the evening of August 16, 1977, to begin another tour. That afternoon, Ginger Alden discovered him unresponsive on his bathroom floor. Attempts to revive him failed, and death was officially pronounced at 3:30 p.m. at Baptist Memorial Hospital.

President Jimmy Carter issued a statement that credited Presley with having "permanently changed the face of American popular culture". Thousands of people gathered outside Graceland to view the open casket. One of Presley's cousins, Billy Mann, accepted $18,000 to secretly photograph the corpse; the picture appeared on the cover of the National Enquirer's biggest-selling issue ever. Alden struck a $105,000 deal with the Enquirer for her story, but settled for less when she broke her exclusivity agreement. Presley left her nothing in his will.

Presley's funeral was held at Graceland on Thursday, August 18. Outside the gates, a car plowed into a group of fans, killing two women and critically injuring a third. Approximately 80,000 people lined the processional route to Forest Hill Cemetery, where Presley was buried next to his mother. Within a few days, "Way Down" topped the country and UK pop charts.

Following an attempt to steal the singer's body in late August, the remains of both Presley and his mother were reburied in Graceland's Meditation Garden on October 2.

Since his death, there have been numerous alleged sightings of Presley. A long-standing theory among some fans is that he faked his death. Fans have noted alleged discrepancies in the death certificate, reports of a wax dummy in his original coffin and numerous accounts of Presley planning a diversion so he could retire in peace.

Questions over cause of death

"Drug use was heavily implicated" in Presley's death, writes Guralnick. "No one ruled out the possibility of anaphylactic shock brought on by the codeine pills ... to which he was known to have had a mild allergy." A pair of lab reports filed two months later each strongly suggested that polypharmacy was the primary cause of death; one reported "fourteen drugs in Elvis' system, ten in significant quantity." Forensic historian and pathologist Michael Baden views the situation as complicated: "Elvis had had an enlarged heart for a long time. That, together with his drug habit, caused his death. But he was difficult to diagnose; it was a judgment call."

The competence and ethics of two of the centrally involved medical professionals were seriously questioned. Before the autopsy was complete and toxicology results known, medical examiner Dr. Jerry Francisco declared the cause of death as cardiac arrhythmia, a condition that can be determined only in someone who is still alive. Allegations of a cover-up were widespread. While Presley's main physician, Dr. Nichopoulos, was exonerated of criminal liability for the singer's death, the facts were startling: "In the first eight months of 1977 alone, he had [prescribed] more than 10,000 doses of sedatives, amphetamines and narcotics: all in Elvis's name." His license was suspended for three months. It was permanently revoked in the 1990s after the Tennessee Medical Board brought new charges of over-prescription.

Amidst mounting pressure in 1994, the Presley autopsy was reopened. Coroner Dr. Joseph Davis declared, "There is nothing in any of the data that supports a death from drugs. In fact, everything points to a sudden, violent heart attack." Whether or not combined drug intoxication was in fact the cause, there is little doubt that polypharmacy contributed significantly to Presley's premature death.

Since 1977

Between 1977 and 1981, six posthumously released singles by Presley were top ten country hits. Graceland was opened to the public in 1982. Attracting over half a million visitors annually, it is the second most-visited home in the United States, after the White House. It was declared a National Historic Landmark in 2006.

Presley has been inducted into five music halls of fame: the Rock and Roll Hall of Fame (1986), the Country Music Hall of Fame (1998), the Gospel Music Hall of Fame (2001), the Rockabilly Hall of Fame (2007), and the Memphis Music Hall of Fame (2012). In 1984, he received the W. C. Handy Award from the Blues Foundation and the Academy of Country Music's first Golden Hat Award. In 1987, he received the American Music Awards' Award of Merit.

A Junkie XL remix of Presley's "A Little Less Conversation" (credited as "Elvis Vs JXL") was used in a Nike advertising campaign during the 2002 FIFA World Cup. It topped the charts in over 20 countries, and was included in a compilation of Presley's number one hits, ELV1S, that was also an international success. In 2003, a remix of "Rubberneckin'", a 1969 recording of Presley's, topped the

U.S. sales chart, as did a 50th-anniversary re-release of "That's All Right" the following year. The latter was an outright hit in the UK, reaching number three on the pop chart.

In 2005, another three reissued singles, "Jailhouse Rock", "One Night"/"I Got Stung", and "It's Now or Never", went to number one in the United Kingdom. A total of 17 Presley singles were reissued during the year; all made the British top five. For the fifth straight year, Forbes named Presley the top-earning deceased celebrity, with a gross income of $45 million. He placed second in 2006, returned to the top spot the next two years, and ranked fourth in 2009. The following year, he was ranked second, with his highest annual income ever—$60 million—spurred by the celebration of his 75th birthday and the launch of Cirque du Soleil's Viva Elvis show in Las Vegas. In November 2010, Viva Elvis: The Album was released, setting his voice to newly recorded instrumental tracks. As of mid-2011, there were an estimated 15,000 licensed Presley products. He was again the second-highest-earning deceased celebrity.

Presley holds the records for most songs charting in Billboard's top 40 and top 100: chart statistician Joel Whitburn calculates the respective totals as 104 and 151; Presley historian Adam Victor gives 114 and 138. Presley's rankings for top-ten and number-one hits vary depending on how the double-sided "Hound Dog/Don't Be Cruel" and "Don't/I Beg of You" singles, which precede the inception of Billboard's unified Hot 100 chart, are analyzed. According to Whitburn's analysis, Presley and Madonna share the record for most top ten hits with 38; per

Billboard's current assessment, he ranks second with 36. Whitburn and Billboard concur that the Beatles hold the record for most number-one hits with 20, and that Mariah Carey is second with 18. Whitburn has Presley also with 18, and thus tied for second; Billboard has him third with 17. Presley retains the record for cumulative weeks at number one: alone at 80, according to Whitburn and the Rock and Roll Hall of Fame; tied with Carey at 79, according to Billboard. He holds the records for most British number-one hits with 21, and top-ten hits with 76. In 2016, the album The Wonder of You, which sets Presley's vocals against music by the Royal Philharmonic Orchestra, was released and reached No. 1 in the UK in October. According to Billboard, this created two new records for Presley: with 13 UK No. 1 albums (The Beatles's total is 15), he is the solo artist with the most number one albums, and the album set a new record for "the longest span between No.1 albums in the UK": Presley first charted at No.1 in 1956 with his self-titled debut album.

In 2008, an 1800-year-old Roman bust described as bearing a "striking" resemblance to Elvis was displayed ahead of an intended auction. A spokesman for the auctioneers said that fans could "be forgiven for thinking that their idol may well have lived a previous life in Rome."

On the anniversary date of his death, every year since 1997, thousands of people gather at his home in Memphis to celebrate his memory, during a candlelight ritual.

Printed in Great Britain
by Amazon

84701859R00031